Devotions for the Engaged Couple

MORE THAN
"I Do"

By HAROLD IVAN SMITH

BEACON HILL PRESS OF KANSAS CITY
KANSAS CITY, MISSOURI

Permission to quote from the following copyrighted versions of the Bible is acknowledged with appreciation:

The Holy Bible, New International Version (NIV), copyright © 1978 by New York International Bible Society.

The *Revised Standard Version of the Bible* (RSV), copyrighted 1946, 1952, © 1971, 1973.

10 9 8 7 6 5 4 3 2 1

Preface

"Something old, something new, something borrowed, something blue" is a cliché that has particular meaning for brides and grooms. We've just gone through a period of time when couples wanted to write their own vows, construct their own ceremonies, initiate new traditions.

Many couples still chose the traditional vows, the timeless. We're not sure when some of the historic words of the vows originated, but across 500 or more years, they've been spoken through tears, through smiles, through the haze and daze of love and romance.

In order to help you become more familiar with these ageless words and phrases, we have taken a phrase a day for a devotional, adding scripture, a definition, and a brief meditation and prayer.

We've also provided a space for you to jot down some thoughts about what the particular phrase means to you. Some days it will be tempting with your hectic schedule to skip over the assignment. But, by the same token, a few minutes a day in the weeks before your wedding will make vows much more meaningful.

The Psalmist long ago declared:

Let the words of my mouth
and the meditation of my heart
be acceptable in thy sight, O Lord, my . . .
Redeemer.

Meditating on your marriage vows would be a super way to begin your transition. Then, a year from now, or a decade from now, take time to reflect again on the fresh meaning of these vows.

✌ DEARLY BELOVED ✌

We are gathered together here in the sight of God, and in the presence of these witnesses, to join together this man and this woman in holy matrimony, which is an honorable estate, instituted of God in the time of man's innocency, signifying unto us the mystical union that exists between Christ and His Church. This holy estate Christ adorned and beautified with His presence and first miracle that He wrought, in Cana of Galilee, and St. Paul commended as being honorable among all men. It is, therefore, not to be entered into unadvisedly, but reverently, discreetly, and in the fear of God.

Into this holy estate these persons present now come to be joined. . . .

Will you have this woman to be your wedded wife, to live together after God's ordinance in the holy estate of matrimony? Will you love her, comfort her, honor and keep her, in sickness and in health; and, forsaking all others, keep yourself only unto her, so long as you both shall live? . . .

Will you have this man to be your wedded husband, to live together after God's ordinance in the holy estate of matrimony? Will you love, honor, and keep him, in sickness and in health; and, forsaking all others, keep yourself only unto him, so long as you both shall live? . . .

Who gives this woman to be married to this man?

I, _____, take you, _____, to be my wedded wife/husband, to have and to hold from this day forward, for better—for worse, for richer—for poorer, in sickness and in health, to love and to cherish, till death us do part, according to God's holy ordinance; and thereto I pledge you my faith. . . .

This ring I give you as a token of my love and as a pledge of my constant fidelity. . . .

Forasmuch as this man and this woman have consented together in holy wedlock, and have witnessed the same before God and this company, and have declared the same by joining of hands, I pronounce that they are husband and wife together, in the name of the Father, and of the Son, and of the Holy Spirit. Those whom God has joined together let not man put asunder. AMEN.

1

Phrase: *"We are gathered together here in the sight of God . . ."*

Text: "Moses did as the Lord commanded him; and the assembly was gathered together unto the door of the tabernacle of the congregation" (Lev. 8:4).

Definition: gather, v 1. to bring into one place or group. 2. come together; assemble. 3. get together from various places or sources.[1]

Idea: The first phrase of the wedding ceremony announces why we will have assembled, although surely everyone knows. We will have come from various places—some coming from quite a distance to participate in this high moment. But we're also coming from various perspectives on marriage. Ideally, marriage is a daily, unfolding splendor, and God can use your wedding to bring fresh thinking to the minds of your family members and other guests. They have gathered to witness a religious moment, an ideal time to reaffirm their own vows and reevaluate their relationships with others and with God.

Many of your guests will find the vows familiar, but they will be fresh and original to you. Think them through, so you can speak them with meaning. "In the sight of God" is an acknowledgment of the Lord's presence. The One who presided at the first wedding in Eden is as anxious to witness yours. We marry in His sight and in His sight we must make a commitment to keep our vows.

Prayer: Father, we're not just tipping our hat to society and doing things the way "they're supposed to be." Keep us aware of You through the 1,001 details that would crowd in and tend to crowd You out. Amen.

WHAT DOES THIS PHRASE MEAN TO YOU?

2

PHRASE: "*... and in the presence of these witnesses ...*"

TEXT: "Every matter must be established by the testimony of two or three witnesses" (2 Cor. 13:1, NIV).

DEFINITION: witness, *n*   1. person or thing able to give evidence; person who saw something happen.

IDEA: The State and the Church both require witnesses to the wedding. It's part of a tradition of remembering. We take the vows more seriously because of the witnesses. For centuries before licenses or documents were developed, the witnesses were the "proof" of the marriage.

Think about your guest list. Family and special friends will be there at your invitation; you want to include them in this special moment of your life. For many it is so important they will rearrange their schedules or travel a long distance to be there. And everyone brings memories of you in other settings: childhood, adolescence, etc. Some will think back to their wedding day.

Those close to you emotionally will probably be the closest to you physically—parents on the front row; friends as attendants.

You could have run off and had this moment only for yourselves, but you have chosen to invest in sharing your joy with others, as you will on many future occasions. Somehow it wouldn't be the same in some neon-flashing, all-night wedding chapel with plastic flowers, taped music, and a "marrying Sam."

In this moment, you will lead us in an act of worship.

PRAYER: Father, this day, help us to consider our witness. There are those who are carefully watching our plans. May they see in all that we do our love for You! Amen.

WHAT DOES THIS PHRASE SAY TO YOU?

PHRASE: "... *to join together this man and this woman in holy matrimony* ..."

TEXT: "He has made everything beautiful in its time" (Eccles. 3:11, RSV).

DEFINITION: join, *v*   1. to place together; combine; connect; fasten; 2. to make into one; unite.[2]

matrimony, *n*   1. the act of marrying; rite or sacrament of marriage. 2. the state of being husband and wife.

IDEA: "To join together *this* man and *this* woman ..." Although millions of couples have pronounced these historic words, they still apply to a specific couple—you!

You are being joined into a new relationship. It's more than putting your clothes in the closet, your name on the mailbox, your toothbrush in the bathroom. You are becoming one. The physical act is too precious to be shared, so the church has recognized this ceremony as an appropriate means to witness and celebrate your new relationship.

For centuries theologians have argued over what precisely creates marriage: coitus or consent. We believe it is both. The vows are a launching; a thousand and one other acts will finalize the process.

Among those who have been "one" for many years, there comes even a spiritual and psychological oneness: they think alike, they may even look alike. Such is the impact of God's best for our lives.

"This man and this woman" is you. Let the vows take on a specific meaning for you!

PRAYER: Father, it's hard to believe that we are "this man and this woman." Give us a sensitive awareness of the vows we are making, that we might be a couple that lifts marriage to be what You intended it to be. Amen.

WHAT DOES THIS PHRASE SAY TO YOU?

PHRASE: *". . . which is an honorable estate . . ."*

TEXT: ". . . hypocritical liars . . . forbid people to marry and order them to abstain from certain foods, which God created to be

10

received with thanksgiving by those who believe and who know the truth. For everything God created is good, and nothing is to be rejected if it is received with thanksgiving, because it is consecrated by the word of God and prayer" (1 Tim. 4:2-5, NIV).

DEFINITION: honorable, *adj*   1. having or showing a sense of what is right and proper; honest; upright. 2. causing honor; bringing honor to the one who has it. 3. worthy of honor; to be respected; noble.

IDEA: These words must be understood in their historic context. In the early days of the church, celibacy, or the rejection of marriage, came to be seen as a "higher" calling. Married people were harangued from the pulpit, denied the sacraments, forced to undergo abstinence . . . until the Reformation.

Then, men like Martin Luther (who married a nun at age 42) and Calvin (who married a widow) sought to restore marriage as part of God's design.

> Luther took the position that the life of marriage offered opportunities for the cultivation of spiritual qualities that were equivalent to those available to the celibate.[3]

> The common men were not theologians and could not defend themselves. The majority could not even read to discover on their own the biblical framework for marriage. You have that advantage. Use it.

PRAYER: Father, what can we do today that will make our approaching wedding and marriage be what You wish it to be? Amen.

WHAT DOES THIS PHRASE MEAN TO YOU?

5

PHRASE: "... *instituted of God in the time of man's innocency* ..."

TEXT: "Then the Lord God said, 'It is not good that the man should be alone; I will make him a helper fit for him'" (Gen. 2:18, RSV).

DEFINITION: instituted, *v*   1. to set up; establish; found; introduce.

IDEA: God is the Designer of marriage. He realized that it was not good for man to be alone. But of all the animals and beasts and birds "there was not found a helper fit for him." God's design was intricate—not "just anything" would do.

Seldom do we praise God for His gift and design; we take our need for a mate for granted. If only that innocency could be rediscovered. "They were both naked . . . and were not ashamed" (v. 25). When they sinned, they found fig leaves to hide from God and from each other.

Sidney Jourard has suggested that "we've shifted the fig leaves from the genitals to our hearts." Today, we don't want people to know how we feel.[4]

Marriage is a tough, demanding process. After the Fall, God did not throw out the institution because Adam and Eve failed. Perhaps you—together—can strive to bring your marriage to God's original intent.

PRAYER: Father, we're not innocent. We've failed You in many ways. But we come to marriage expectantly—help us to discover the wonder of Your unique gift! Amen.

WHAT DOES THIS PHRASE SAY TO YOU?

6

PHRASE: *". . . signifying unto us the mystical union that exists between Christ and His Church."*

TEXT: "For the husband is the head of the wife as Christ is the head of the church, his body, of which he is the Savior. Now as the church submits to Christ, so also wives should submit to their husbands in everything. Husbands, love your wives, just as Christ loved the church and gave himself up for her to make her holy" (Eph. 5:23-26, NIV).

DEFINITION: signifying, *v*   1. be a sign of; mean.

IDEA: Of all the examples the sacred writers could have used to explain the relationship between Christ and the Church, under the guidance of the Holy Spirit, they chose marriage. The New Testament writers were familiar with the prophets who had used the relationship to symbolize God's relation to Israel. The minor prophetic passages portrayed God as a wounded husband grieving over the mate's unfaithfulness.

In the New Testament, God could have chosen a new metaphor to illustrate the new covenant, but He chose to keep the old one.

Thus, God insists that marriage be pure—otherwise, it tarnishes our theological imagery, which would make it difficult to comprehend our relationship to Him.

The Church is the Bride of Christ and the Book of Revelation is filled with wedding allegories.

Your task, today and in all the days of your marriage, is to keep the metaphor valid in your life.

PRAYER: Father, in the relationship of husband and wife, You have chosen US to be an example of the believer's relationship to You. Help us to protect that meaning against anything that would tarnish it. Amen.

WHAT DOES THIS PHRASE MEAN TO YOU?

7

PHRASE: *"This holy estate Christ adorned and beautified with His presence and first miracle that He wrought, in Cana of Galilee..."*

TEXT: "The master of the banquet tasted the water that had been turned into wine. He did not realize where it had come from, though the servants who had drawn the water knew. Then he called the bridegroom aside and said, 'Everyone brings out the choice wine first and then the cheaper wine after the guests have had too much to drink; but you have saved the best till now'" (John 2:9-10, NIV).

DEFINITION: adorn, *v*   1. add beauty to; make greater the splendor or honor of.

IDEA: What a man does speaks more clearly than what he says. It is somewhat ironic that Jesus—a never-married man— began His public ministry at a wedding. Coincidence? or design?

What is significant in this passage is the effect the miracle had on His disciples: "He thus revealed his glory, and his disciples put their faith in him" (John 2:11, NIV).

14

Your ceremony is your last event as a single—your first experience as a married person. You will be changed just as certainly as the water that went into the seven jars came out wine. In our thinking, marriage is not a sacrament but is *sacramental*—an opportunity for grace to occur.

And you can live your marriage in such a way that all who see it will recognize it as the best.

PRAYER: Father, as through Your grace the water was turned into wine, may we be changed from single adults into a married couple. May our witness be of the "best" of marriage. Amen.

WHAT DOES THIS PHRASE SAY TO YOU?

PHRASE: ". . . *and St. Paul commended as being honorable among all men.*"

TEXT: "Since there is so much immorality, each man should have his own wife, and each woman her own husband. The husband should fulfill his marital duty to his wife, and likewise the wife to her husband" (1 Cor. 7:2-3, NIV).

DEFINITION: commend, *v*   2. to mention as worthy of regard; recommend. 3. to praise.

IDEA: Marriage is not just for Christians. Paul insisted it is "honorable" among all men. Wherever Christian faith has gone, it has worked to raise the image of marriage—even when it meant a collision course with existing culture.

Since time began, philosophers and free thinkers have advanced theories and notions, and a variety of marriage and kinship patterns have emerged. Today, live-ins have grown by 300 percent in the last decade; they want the better, the richer, health, and "sex."[5] Some no doubt pride themselves on their avant-garde life-styles.

But there are those people who seek marriage even though they do not yet know the God who created it. Indeed, some non-Christians have made and are making more of their marriages than some believers. Unholy deadlock is a tragic alternative to holy wedlock: you must make the choice.

The Roman civilization collapsed when it accommodated the unhonorable. That stands as a warning to any culture that permits encroachments on the sanctity of marriage.

PRAYER: Father, Your Word affirms that everything You made You pronounced "good." Help us to live our marriage in such a way that it will be acceptable and honorable in Your sight. This we ask through Him who gives us strength. Amen.

WHAT DOES THIS PHRASE SAY TO YOU?

PHRASE: *"It is, therefore, not to be entered into unadvisedly . . ."*

TEXT: "Only by pride cometh contention: but with the well advised is wisdom" (Prov. 13:10).

DEFINITION: advisedly, *adv*   after careful consideration; deliberately.

IDEA: Paul advised young Timothy, to "Watch your life and doctrine closely" (1 Tim. 4:16, NIV). There must be no contradiction between what we believe and what we do, for we are modeling our life-style and values to a world hostile to faith and skeptical of the institution of marriage.

Paul certainly recognized the exuberance of youth. It's easy to get wrapped up in the daily affairs of life. It's also natural to desire marriage: a home, companionship, even a family. But if that desire balloons and is not disciplined, we lose our objectivity. The enemy will use *anything*—even a marriage—to limit or nullify our witness.

John Wesley once preached against marriage for his young Methodist preachers. However, not three weeks later, he himself married a woman he hardly knew and suffered an immediate estrangement from his brother Charles. The marriage was unwise and proved to be an embarrassment when the woman released some of his private letters to his critics.

This great saint suffered because of his marriage. If he made a mistake, so can you. Seek the advice of others and seek God's best for your life. Our *Manual* insists that marriage be entered into only after "earnest prayer."

Some people do not invest enough thought and commitment in decision-making: They reason that if what they have selected proves to be not to their liking, it can be replaced. Remember, your choice of a mate is for a lifetime—"till death us do part."

Part of the advice-gathering process is premarital counseling. It is one of the wisest investments you can make.

PRAYER: Father, have we asked only that You "OK" our decision to marry? Have we asked only that You "OK" the 1,001 details? Are we asking You "to go along with" our decisions and choices? We need to know Your will and the courage to be obedient to that will. Amen.

What Does This Phrase Mean to You?

10

Phrase: *"... but reverently ..."*

Text: "Therefore, since we are receiving a kingdom that cannot be shaken, let us be thankful, and so worship God acceptably with reverence and awe, for our God is a consuming fire" (Heb. 12:28-29, NIV).

Definition: reverence, *n*   1. a feeling of deep respect, mixed with wonder, awe, and love.

Idea: Have you ever been accused of being irreverent or sacrilegious? There's a sting to the charge and we're quick to point out that was not our intent.

A wedding is to be reverent. In ancient times, the ceremonies lasted for days, with lively celebration. During the Reformation, John Calvin forbade singing and dancing at Puritan weddings.

Christians have strengthened the significance of weddings. The weddings of the first century were quite secular, with a sacrifice and prayers to a pagan god. Christians added the celebration of the Eucharist—the sharing of holy Communion.

For many couples their first act as husband and wife is to take Communion, an act of worship that acknowledges our awe of God as well as submission to His leading in our lives.

Guard against anything in your wedding that would tarnish the reverence. The music is to glorify God. And that can be taken a bit too far. One groom sang, "I'd Rather Have Jesus."

A wedding can be a holy celebration of worship! It's a dimension that can be experienced only in a Christian wedding.

PRAYER: Father, it is possible to lose sight of You amid all the plans and details. We would have You as our Guest, not just at our wedding but throughout our marriage. Make us more sensitive to Your guidance and direction in our lives. Amen.

WHAT DOES THIS PHRASE SAY TO YOU?

11

PHRASE: ". . . *discreetly* . . ."

TEXT: "Teach the young women . . . to be discreet, chaste, keepers at home, good, obedient to their own husbands, that the word of God be not blasphemed" (Titus 2:4*a*, 5).

DEFINITION: discretion, *n*   1. freedom to judge or choose. 2. good judgment; carefulness in speech and action; wise caution.

IDEA: In many cultures of the world, marriages are arranged. Families insist that marriage is too important to society to allow it to be based on such a fleeting notion as romance. Sometimes the bride and groom do not even know each other. Because of the strong sanctions of such a society, divorce is unthinkable.

In our society, you have been given the freedom to choose, although inherent within that freedom is the opportunity to choose the wrong person, or the right person for the wrong reasons.

Is your choice of a marriage partner wise? Is your timing for marriage wise? So many are in love with love rather than with a person. While you are planning the wedding you are center-stage—after all, it's your "big day."

Tragically, in too many cases, there are people raising questions about the choice or timing, although most would never express their questions or reservations to the couple.

It would be tragic if you—with so much freedom of choice—would make a bad choice:

to prove something to someone . . .

to defy . . .

to rebound.

Make a good choice, because it is a life choice—until death.

PRAYER: Father, love can be so wonderful, so joyous—but it can also be like a fog—so thick that we cannot see the dangerous rocks. You allowed me to be born in a culture where marital choice prevails. Enable me to make the choice according to Your will for my life. Amen.

WHAT DOES THIS PHRASE MEAN TO YOU?

12

PHRASE: *"... and in the fear of God."*

TEXT: "The fear of the Lord is the beginning of wisdom: a good understanding have all they that do his commandments: his praise endureth for ever" (Ps. 111:10).

DEFINITION: fear, *n*   1. being afraid; feeling that danger or evil is near; dread. 3. an uneasy feeling; anxious thought. 4. awe; reverence.

IDEA: *Fear* is a tough word, a word often shunted to the back burners of our vocabularies. However, the Word insists, "The fear of the Lord is the beginning of wisdom." What better scripture could comfort you as you begin your marriage?

Some people turn to God in times of trouble; in the good times they rely on their own strength. But He wants to be God in the good times as well as the bad.

Fearing God does not mean God is there waiting to swat you with His big stick. *Fear* in this case means that you respect Him and want to please Him. He is as anxious to be evident at your wedding as He was at Cana in Galilee.

Can't you see His leading in your lives that has brought you to this place?

One gospel songwriter observed,

> He leadeth me! Oh blessed tho't!
> Oh, words with heav'nly comfort fraught!
> Whate'er I do, where'er I be,
> Still 'tis God's hand that leadeth me.
>
> He leadeth me, He leadeth me.
> By His own hand He leadeth me.

21

His faithful follower I would be
For by His hand He leadeth me.
—Joseph H. Gilmore

PRAYER: Father, we would like to come to You as children. We are aware of the many ways You have led and *are* leading in our lives. Continue to lead us so that our marriage will be Your best for our lives. Amen.

WHAT DOES THIS PHRASE MEAN TO YOU?

13

PHRASE: *"Will you have this woman/man to be your wedded wife/husband . . . ?"*

TEXT: "Laban brought together all the people of the place and gave a feast. But when evening came, he took his daughter Leah and gave her to Jacob. . . . When morning came, there was Leah!" (Gen. 29:22-23*a*, 25, NIV).

DEFINITION: this, *adj*   1. the person, thing, event, quality, condition, idea, etc., that is present, mentioned, or referred to now.

IDEA: You are not making vows of commitment to just anyone—but to a specific man or woman. His or her name, face, and personality have become special to you. Martin Buber, a Jewish theologian, talked about the one we love as the "thou"—too special to be a "you."

In arranged weddings, the groom might never have seen the woman (or vice versa) until the day of the wedding. Jacob was tricked by his father-in-law. He thought he was marrying Rachel, but had a rude awakening the next morning. The King James says it so starkly: "Behold, it was Leah."

The wedding veil is symbolic of the differences you will see after the wedding, as marriage gradually unfolds and you discover much more about this person you have married.

We marry specific people—therefore, it behoves us to know as much about them as possible *before* we marry.

The vows you will make are not to marriage in general, but to a specific person. Make them wisely.

PRAYER: Father, before long we will repeat our marriage vows. Help us to be certain that the "wills" we are making reflect Your will for our lives. Keep us aware of the importance of decisions we are making. Amen.

WHAT DOES THIS PHRASE MEAN TO YOU?

14

PHRASE: "... *to live together after God's ordinance in the holy estate of matrimony.*"

TEXT: "I know that whatever God does endures for ever; nothing can be added to it, nor anything taken from it; God has made it so, in order that men should fear before him" (Eccles. 3:14, RSV).

IDEA: We have a lot of teaching on marriage: books, seminars, records, tapes, sermons, pamphlets—sometimes offering opinions that conflict or confuse. But ordinance is singular. Why?

Because at the heart of Scripture, God's design is plain. Three times passages begin, *"for this reason* a man will leave his father and mother and be united to his wife, and the two will become one flesh" (Gen. 2:24; Matt. 19:5; Eph. 5:31, NIV, italics added).

Nothing is to interfere with the marital relationship. We must understand these verses in the light of a culture that was composed of extended families—more than one generation under the roof.

We are to live as husband and wife in ways that enhance our oneness.

Whatever you still need to *leave* in order to *cleave* must be done! Honoring your mate is a higher priority than honoring your parents.

PRAYER: Father, we want to be all that You want us to be. We want to obey Your ordinance in order to obtain Your richest blessings upon our marriage. Open our eyes to submerged issues that could hurt our relationship with each other and with You. Amen.

WHAT DOES THIS PHRASE MEAN TO YOU?

15

Phrase: *"Will you love her/him . . . ?"*

Text: "Love is patient, love is kind. It does not envy, it does not boast, it is not proud. It is not rude, it is not self-seeking, it is not easily angered, it keeps no record of wrongs. Love does not delight in evil but rejoices in the truth. It always protects, always trusts, always hopes, always perseveres" (1 Cor. 13:4-7, NIV).

Definition: will, *v*   1. decide by using the power of the mind to decide and to do; use the will. 3. determine.

Idea: Love is a decision. But it is a confused word in today's world: we love baseball, and hot dogs, and the Dallas Cowboys. . . . The apostle Paul wrote some of the most touching words in any mortal tongue when he wrote 1 Corinthians 13, "the love chapter."

Consider the following . . .

LOVE is patient. . . . Am I patient?
LOVE is kind. . . . Am I kind?
LOVE does not envy. . . . Do I envy?
LOVE does not boast. . . . Do I boast? If so, what about?
LOVE is not proud. . . . Am I proud?
LOVE is not rude. . . . Am I rude?
LOVE is not self-seeking. . . . Am I ever self-seeking, wanting my way?
LOVE is not easily angered. . . . Am I too easily angered?
LOVE keeps no record of wrongs. . . . Do I keep a record of wrongs?

LOVE does not delight in evil. . . . Do I chuckle over the wrongs of others?

LOVE rejoices in the truth. . . . Do I rejoice in the truth?

LOVE always protects. . . . Do I protect my fiancé/fiancée?

LOVE always trusts. . . . Do I trust my fiancé/fiancée totally?

LOVE always hopes. . . . Do I?

LOVE always perseveres. . . . Will our love endure?

Perhaps it would make more sense if we asked in the ceremony, "Do you love him/her? *now?*—and more than yesterday?" Too many have gone into marriage, hoping to fall into love—hoping the feeling will be there. Some have anesthetized doubts or warning signals. Do you really love your fiancé/fiancée?

PRAYER: Father, our thoughts, our wishes, our intents—are open to You. We have said we love. Deliver us from worldly misdefinitions of the word. Examine our hearts and help us to love as You would have us love. Give me the strength to love in such a way that Your definition of love will be modeled to others through our lives. Amen.

WHAT DOES THIS PHRASE MEAN TO YOU?

16

PHRASE: *". . . comfort her . . ."*

TEXT: "Isaac brought her into his mother Sarah's tent, and took Rebekah, and she became his wife; and he loved her: and Isaac was comforted after his mother's death" (Gen. 24:67).

DEFINITION: comfort, *v*   1. ease the grief or sorrow of; cheer. *n*   3. person or thing that makes life easier or takes away hardships.

IDEA: A hundred years ago, a couple could expect as a wedding present a comforter—an extra bed covering for those especially cold nights. My grandmother made a comforter in the Dutch Boy pattern for each of her grandsons. Today it is a valued possession.

Marriage was designed for the mutual comfort of man and woman. At a wedding we focus on the joys of wedding. In ancient Jewish ceremonies, however, the couple sipped wine from a goblet. Then the goblet was placed on the floor and crushed to symbolize the other dimensions of marriage—the sorrows and griefs.

The God who said, "It is not good for the man to be alone" brings a partner to make life easier or take away the hardships—or to go through them with him.

The story is told of a first-time runner in the Boston Marathon. By a certain point in the race he was barely running, his muscles were cramping, and he was crying. The crowd urged him to continue. Out of the pack came another runner who sensed the man's need. He ran up to him and put his arm around the struggling runner's waist and urged him on—hip to hip. The older, more mature runner became a

27

comforter to the other man. As a result, both finished the Marathon.

It is possible in difficult times to draw closer to each other! Doing so will make the joyous days even more joyous.

PRAYER: Father, we have already felt the comfort of each other's love. In the days and months and years ahead, help us to comfort one another freely. We do not ask that You spare us the hardships of life but only that You give us the grace to experience them together. Amen.

WHAT DOES THIS PHRASE MEAN TO YOU?

17

PHRASE: *". . . honor and keep her/him . . ."*

TEXT: "'Honor your father and mother'—which is the first commandment with a promise—'that it may go well with you and that you may enjoy long life on the earth'" (Eph. 6:2-3, NIV).

DEFINITION: honor, *v*   1. respect greatly; regard highly. 2. show respect to. 3. worship.

IDEA: We tend to associate "honor" with our parents as in the Ten Commandments, "Honor your father and mother" (Deut. 5:16). With that commandment there was a promise: that our days would be long upon the earth.

Violence in families is a growing cause of concern in our society. Wife-beating, husband-beating, and child-beating are

28

all too prevalent. Severe injury and deaths occur among those who do not "greatly respect" their mate. Oh, some of us would never "lay a finger on them" but our words can wound and maim just as effectively.

In a real sense we honor a mate by honoring *all* the vows of the wedding ceremony. Work creatively in honoring your mate. Engagement should be an apprenticeship in honoring each other.

In what ways do you honor your fiancé/fiancée? Paul advised the Romans, "Love must be sincere. Hate what is evil; cling to what is good. . . . Honor one another above your-selves" (Rom. 12:9-10, NIV). If he said that about brotherly love, how much more would he say it about marital love?

PRAYER: Father, help us to realize how pleased You are when we honor our vows. But help us also to realize that to honor another is work and must be a daily commitment, not a remembrance on our anniversaries and birthdays. Teach us how to honor each other. Amen.

WHAT DOES THIS PHRASE MEAN TO YOU?

18

PHRASE: "*. . . in sickness and in health . . .*"

TEXT: "The Lord will sustain him on his sickbed and restore him from his bed of illness" (Ps. 41:3, NIV).

DEFINITION: health, *n*   1. physical and mental wellbeing;

soundness; freedom from defect, pain, or disease; normality of mental and physical functions.

IDEA: Whoever composed the vows placed the negative (sickness) first as a reality. When these vows were first spoken, few couples celebrated their 25th wedding anniversaries—death at an early age was all too common, particularly through childbirth. Medicine was a primitive art, so sickness could devour families and communities in a single swoop.

Despite advanced technological developments, sickness is still a reality that couples must anticipate—and some saints turn into "bears" when ill.

Illness affects every facet of a marriage and sometimes good health does not return quickly. In a mate's illness, you are vulnerable. Sometimes a mate becomes impatient with illness and its implications. There are special diets, body changes, fatigue—to say nothing of the expense.

Illness also affects the sexual aspect of marriage—and some illness is psychosomatic, brought on by unmet emotional needs. Some find the only way they can gain a mate's attention is through illness. But intimacy must remain. In *Love Story,* one of the most poignant passages of the book came as Jenny was dying of leukemia and she asked Oliver "to hold me."[6] That wasn't sexual, but illustrated the type of profound intimacy that makes marriage "one flesh."

PRAYER: Father, we don't want to be sick. But when those times do come, give us strength to be caring and compassionate, loving and kind. Help us to celebrate our health and to be aware of ways we can promote health and well-being. Amen.

WHAT DOES THIS PHRASE MEAN TO YOU?

19

PHRASE: *". . . and, forsaking all others . . ."*

TEXT: "Marriage should be honored by all, and the marriage bed kept pure, for God will judge the adulterer and all the sexually immoral" (Heb. 13:4, NIV).

DEFINITION: forsaking, *v*   1. give up; leave alone; leave.

IDEA: This phrase seems immediately explainable—no adultery! Acts of infidelity can quickly dissolve the bonds of marriage. Adultery cannot be tolerated because marriage is the example of Christ's relationship to the Church. Could spiritual adultery be accepted? No!

On the other hand, too many have assumed that one act of adultery is automatic grounds for divorce. Adultery scars and maims—but we must forgive. More marriages could be saved if we realized that Jesus' words on forgiveness in Matthew 18 preceded His words on divorce in Matthew 19.

But sometimes it's not people but *things* that become wedges between husband and wife. "Others" could be

- —jobs
- —sports
- —hobbies
- —children
- —animals

The "one flesh" is to be a reality in our lives—exclusively between husband and wife.

Forsaking implies *choosing* to forsake, however demanding that decision may be.

PRAYER: Father, as we want nothing to come between You and us, we ask also that nothing come between us and our love for each other. If, somehow, we begin to tolerate small divisive factors, confront us. Amen.

WHAT DOES THIS PHRASE MEAN TO YOU?

20

PHRASE: *". . . keep yourself only unto her/him, so long as you both shall live."*

TEXT: "Enjoy life with your wife, whom you love, all the days of this meaningless life that God has given you under the sun" (Eccles. 9:9, NIV).

DEFINITION: keep, *v*   1. to observe or pay regard to. 2. to take care of; specifically, *(a)* to protect; guard; defend; *(d)* to maintain in good order or condition; preserve.

IDEA: In an age of do-it-yourself wedding vows, and with a generation that has rarely seen lifelong commitment portrayed, these vows have been modified to read, "as long as we both shall love." It is the ultimate assertion of the "i" (symbolic of the big I), so "live" becomes "love." Some insist this saves them from hypocrisy.

　　As a writer, I receive contracts that on some sections benefit me—others, the publishers. If I don't like a certain provision I "x" it out and sign my initials. But the wedding vows cannot be "x-ed" out even in the age of the disposable, no-deposit, no-return.

Dwight Small observes, "With the acceleration of social change, young people have had little opportunity to experience real stability and permanence. As a result they tend to think of marriage as a process, not a product, as a tentative *now* relationship rather than a life-unifying commitment."[7]

It requires a decision on your part.

PRAYER: Father, it would be tempting to modernize these vows a little bit, to change "live" to "love." But help us to be aware that love is a decision, a choice. Keep us conscious of things or people that would threaten our love. Amen.

WHAT DOES THIS PHRASE MEAN TO YOU?

21

PHRASE: *"Who gives this woman to be married to this man?"*

TEXT: "Laban and Bethuel answered . . . 'Here is Rebekah; take her and go, and let her become the wife of your master's son, as the Lord has directed'" (Gen. 24:50a-51, NIV).

DEFINITION: give, *v*   1. hand over as a present. 2. hand over (a bride) to a bridegroom.

IDEA: Already we can hear the protest "Gives?" A woman is not a possession to be given, traded, or bought—such language is archaic!

Today women are delaying marriage in favor of in-

33

creased educational and professional career opportunities. The percentage of unmarried women in 1960 was 26.5 percent; today it is 39.1 percent.[8] If nothing else, we can celebrate the progress we've made in affirming women. At one time, a woman went from a bedroom in her father's house to a bedroom in her husband's home.

This phrase is to monitor Gen. 2:24, "to leave mother and father." Giving the bride becomes a declaration of "hands off." Too many marriages are hamstrung, if not sabotaged, by interfering in-laws. "Letting go" in the ceremony needs to be more emphasized to both sets of parents.

Finally, this phrase is a recognition that much of what the woman brings to marriage are *givens* from her family—a name, opinions, attitudes, and habits.

And some of those givens—although abstract—will have a significant effect on the potential for success.

PRAYER: Father, today we pray for our parents who have given so much to us. We thank You for their godly lives. Help them to see ways to "let go" and give freely so that our marriage can be blessed by You. Amen.

WHAT DOES THIS PHRASE MEAN TO YOU?

22

PHRASE: *"I take you to be my wedded wife/husband . . ."*

TEXT: "Three things are too wonderful for me; four I do not understand: . . . and the way of a man with a maiden" (Prov. 30:18, 19*b*, RSV).

DEFINITION: take, *v*   5. accept. 6. receive into some relationship.

IDEA: The phrase is one of definite decision, "I take you . . . now." Some people have tacked on conditional clauses:
> —"I take you . . . when you do such and such."
> —"I take you . . . if you promise to do thus and so."

or even,
> —"I take you *because* you do such and such or are such . . ."

Rather, Josh McDowell insists we take a mate, *period*—without qualifications or reservations. We promise to love. Such is a unique blend of agape and eros.[9]

Unfortunately, some marry with an agenda of changes they want or plan to make. They confidently declare, "I can change him/her."

Jason Towner wrote, "I choose you alone from all the world to love and to be faithful to through all the changes of life."[10]

"I take you" means, I *accept* you and "I promise to accept the mystery of your unique being and to love you as you are."

That takes courage—but pays incredible dividends.

PRAYER: Father, it is easy to put in little qualifiers, "if" or "when" or "because." But You have loved us without merit, while we were sinners. Teach us how to love our mates as You would have us love. Amen.

WHAT DOES THIS PHRASE MEAN TO YOU?

23

PHRASE: *". . . to have and to hold from this day forward . . ."*

TEXT: "The Lord God . . . brought her to the man. Then the man said, 'This at last is bone of my bones and flesh of my flesh; she shall be called Woman, because she was taken out of Man'" (Gen. 2:22-23, RSV).

DEFINITION: have, *v*   1. to hold in the hand or in control; own; possess.

IDEA: Clearly, the vow writers were thinking of "hold" as meaning possession. However, early in marriage, the seeds of "taking for granted" are planted.

There doesn't seem to be a lot of holding and caressing after marriage. We've so made intercourse the big event, that we fail to be intimate.

"Hold me" is a basic need for most healthy people. God has endowed our bodies with thousands of touch sensors, filled with tactile mechanisms. To have to *ask* to be held is like asking for a birthday party—definitely not as much fun.

Marriage does grant the green light to full sexual expression in your lives. But don't overlook the luxury of holding hands, of touching, of embracing. Don't give up intimacy for sexuality.

PRAYER: Father, out of all the people I could have loved, I have chosen to love ____ and accept love from him/her. Help me to hold fast to that love and to nourish it in all the days that are ahead. Amen.

WHAT DOES THIS PHRASE MEAN TO YOU?

24

PHRASE: *". . . for better—for worse . . ."*

TEXT: "House and wealth are inherited from fathers, but a prudent wife is from the Lord" (Prov. 19:14, RSV).

DEFINITION: worse, *adj*   1. less well; more ill; 3. more unfavorable.

IDEA:

- "I didn't count on this . . ."
- "This is not part of the bargain . . ."
- "Marriage is a 50-50 proposition . . ."

As a child, did you ever hurt yourself and ask a parent, tearfully, to "make it better"? Now, as an adult, you're full of dreams and hopes and expectations of what marriage, in general, and marriage specifically (with "him" or "her") will be like.

But have you shared these expectations and honestly faced them? Are you agreed? You see, the tendency is to wait until we confront an issue. It's too easy to say, "We'll cross that bridge when we come to it!"

Things change—not necessarily by choice, but by imposition. Some people have talked about "marriage contracts" with clauses and conditions and penalties. This is more a testimony to an exaggerated ego than to Christian faith. Jason Towner wrote, "I promise to love you in all the changes of life."[11]

What's "worse" today is relative. Tomorrow's "worse" may cause you to fondly wish for today's "worse" or yesterday's. Marriage is not some delicate scale in which you try to keep "better" in balance with "worse." Sometimes, when it rains, it pours.

In today's world, it will take 110 percent from each of you to make it work, "for better or for worse."

PRAYER: Father, You do not change. We always want the good-times dimension to marriage; but those "worse" times will come. Please enable us to face them in Your grace with Your help. Cause us to rush to You with our troubles as a child to a father. Amen.

WHAT DOES THIS PHRASE MEAN TO YOU?

25

PHRASE: *"... for richer—for poorer ..."*

DEFINITION: rich, *adj*   1. having much money or property. 2. abundantly supplied with resources.

TEXT: "My God will meet all your needs according to his glorious riches in Christ Jesus" (Phil. 4:19, NIV).

IDEA: How much money will it take to "keep the wolf from your door"? Is the wedding still within its budget or is it growing like the national debt?

Money—there's never enough; the more you make, the more you spend—two common assumptions. With "plastic money" so common a way of life, how will you exercise discipline?

Money destroys a lot of marriages—not simply the lack of it, but the abundance as well.

PORK AND BEANS . . .

It's funny how they tasted so different
  than the way they do now.
What did you put in them to make them taste so
  good?
  Pork and beans—cheap, easy to fix
  once delicious but now so-so.
Why is that?
They tasted so much better before we had the
  money for steak.[12]

Maybe you will have to sacrifice to fertilize your dreams. Remember that *things* don't bring happiness—they only complicate your life.

A top priority of your marriage must be to learn to distinguish between your *needs* and your *wants*. Ask, Do we *really* need this? now? at all?

PRAYER: Father, we'd rather be rich than poor. But we'd rather be what You would want us to be. Help us to remember that money is not the only way to be wealthy. We are rich because of Your love. Amen.

WHAT DOES THIS PHRASE MEAN TO YOU?

26

PHRASE: *". . . to love and to cherish . . ."*

TEXT: "Let there be sought for my lord the king a young virgin:

and let her stand before the king, and let her cherish him" (1 Kings 1:2).

DEFINITION: cherish, *v* 1. to hold dear; treat with affection. 2. care for tenderly. 3. keep in mind; cling to.

IDEA: Someone reportedly asked Billy Graham what he would do if he realized he no longer loved his wife. The evangelist replied, "I'd get down on my knees and begin praying and I wouldn't get up until I either loved her or could act toward her in loving ways!"

Love is a decision-based emotion. So, if you fall into love, it's only reasonable that you could just as easily fall *out* of love. But people don't stop loving—they just stop choosing to love.

Throughout your marriage, there will be high seasons and low seasons of emotion. Regardless of emotions, the Christian makes and keeps a commitment to love.

Sometimes those who say they're no longer in love, simply are not putting love into action. And the testimony of many is that through the Holy Spirit, the dying embers can be stirred into life. The warmth of mature love is a sustaining reality and joy for many today.

To cherish is a special love, a higher form of love not known by beginners. We are to *cherish* our mates. That too is a decision.

PRAYER: Father, we've sung that hymn about cherishing the old rugged Cross. That puts singing or thinking about cherishing our mates on the highest plane. Help us keep this vow, because there surely will be times when only by Your grace and strength will it be possible. Amen.

WHAT DOES THIS PHRASE MEAN TO YOU?

27

PHRASE: *". . . till death us do part . . ."*

TEXT: "Who shall separate us . . .? Shall trouble or hardship or persecution or famine or nakedness or danger or sword?" (Rom. 8:35, NIV).

DEFINITION: part, *v*   1. divide into two or more pieces. 3. force apart; divide.

IDEA: There is always the danger of taking a text out of context. Perhaps your initial response is that this passage refers to our relationship to Christ. And it does.

But Paul told the Ephesians that our relationship with Christ was like the relationship between husband and wife. Can any of these things divide you?

- trouble?
- hardship? (you've promised "for better or worse")
- persecution?
- famine?
- nakedness?
- danger?
- sword?

Paul added that we find our confidence "through him that loved us." Christ can enable us to keep the vows we make.

Some couples today take the attitude, "We're together unless something breaks us up." Other couples, especially live-ins, say *"Until* something breaks us up."

I believe you can agree

> "that neither death nor life,
> neither angels nor demons,
> neither the present nor the future,

nor any powers,
neither height nor depth,
nor anything else in all creation,
will be able to separate us" (vv. 38-39, NIV).

The confidence to vow "till death us do part" is in Him who ordained marriage.

PRAYER: Father, we don't want to think about death. We're just beginning. But You are Alpha and Omega, the beginning and the end. Help us to cherish our days together. Amen.

WHAT DOES THIS PHRASE MEAN TO YOU?

28

PHRASE: "... according to God's holy ordinance..."

TEXT: "The end of the matter; all has been heard. Fear God, and keep his commandments; for this is the whole duty of man" (Eccles. 12:13, RSV).

DEFINITION: ordinance, *n*   1. a direction or command of an authoritative nature. 2. a custom or practice established by usage or authority. 3. an established religious rite.

IDEA: Someone has identified three functions of God's design for marriage.

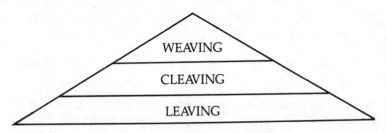

We can leave but neither cleave nor weave;
We can attempt to cleave but never fully leave;
We can weave but never cleave or leave.

Cleaving refers to a process like gluing. There is an ad on television in which a man puts "Crazy Glue" on his hard hat and fastens it under a steel beam. We are stunned that his weight does not pull the hat from the beam. But such is the strength of the glue. (Maybe we should wonder how he keeps his head in his hat!)

God's ordinance is universal for the good of *all* mankind. Those who ignore it do so at their own peril.

PRAYER: Father, help us to take seriously Your ordinance of marriage. Given as a good gift from a loving Father, it is for our benefit. Thank You for being so interested in us. Amen.

WHAT DOES THIS PHRASE MEAN TO YOU?

29

PHRASE: *". . . and thereto I pledge you my faith."*

TEXT: "Husbands should love their wives as their own bodies. He who loves his wife loves himself" (Eph. 5:28, RSV).

DEFINITION: pledge, *v*   1. promise solemnly. 3. give as security.

IDEA: This phrase was originally part of a separate ceremony of betrothal. The archaic form was, "I plight thee my troth."

In contract marriages, penalties for broken promises are clearly stated. In Christian marriage, we can only offer our word and the realization that the Holy Spirit will help us keep our vows.

Sometimes in commercial contracts surety is a requirement whereby people put up money to guarantee their performance. So, if I then fail some part of the agreement, my surety is broken and the wounded person collects payment without suing me. After paying for a wedding and setting up a house or apartment, there's not much left and all some of us ever have is our word.

Paul insisted that marriage symbolized the relationship between Christ and the Church. What does Christ ask that we put up to earn that relationship or to forfeit if we fail? He wants commitment.

The only surety we have in marriage is our commitment. And as Towner insisted: "The promises made at a flower-lined altar are only as good as those made at the altar of our hearts, daily."[13]

PRAYER: Father, I'm planning on taking a vow but sometimes I'm frightened by it. So many others have taken the same vows but have not kept them. Help me to keep my vow daily—and hourly if need be. Amen.

WHAT DOES THIS PHRASE MEAN TO YOU?

30

PHRASE: *"This ring I give you as a token of my love ..."*

TEXT: "The father said to his servants, 'Quick! Bring the best robe and put it on him. Put a ring on his finger and sandals on his feet. Bring the fattened calf. . . . For this son of mine was dead and is alive again'" (Luke 15:22-24, NIV).

DEFINITION: token, *n*   1. something serving to indicate some fact, feeling, event; mark or sign. 2. keepsake; 4. piece of metal indicating a right or privilege.

IDEA: In mankind's early history, barter was the chief form of business. Precious metals (gold and silver) came into acceptance as tokens. But rather than just carrying their money, people wore it in jewelry: rings, chains, etc. If they could not strike a barter exchange—they gave a link of their gold chain or other token.

The Romans used rings to seal the betrothal. It was an outward sign of an inward act of consent. Abraham's servant exchanged jewelry with Laban before he took Rebekah.

You wear a ring to signal your engagement, which is translated "token." Later, you will receive a wedding band to complement it.

Unfortunately, wedding bands can be "slipped off," but many people *never* remove them. Although you may prosper financially, this ring will always be special.

Rings signify relationships. When the prodigal son returned, his father called for a ring to symbolize his new relationship.

As the ring is of precious material, so is your love. As the ring is endless, so is your love.

PRAYER: Father, You designed marriage and You designed all the precious metals. You also have designed that relationships become precious. Thank You for the richness of all of Your gifts to us. Don't let me fail to recognize the beauty of them. Amen.

WHAT DOES THIS PHRASE MEAN TO YOU?

31

PHRASE: *". . . and as a pledge of my constant fidelity."*

TEXT: "I will betroth you to me forever; I will betroth you in righteousness and justice, in love and compassion. I will betroth you in faithfulness" (Hos. 2:19-20, NIV).

DEFINITION: constant, *adj*   1. always the same; not changing. 2. never stopping. 4. faithful, loyal.

IDEA: In certain aspects of mathematics, there are constants. In navigation, the degrees of longitude and latitude are not changeable. Greenwich time is the basis for standard time throughout the world. There are things that do not change although change is occurring all about us.

Fidelity has to be a constant commitment; idle or slack moments can be disastrous. Often we have the notion that marriages *suddenly* fell apart. Not so. An editorial in *Dads Only* observed:

No man suddenly decides to divorce his wife. The actual decision is invariably the sordid fruit of stray thoughts cultivated rather than rooted out over a period of time. Lingering glances at other women, a subtle, secret enjoyment of certain types of publications, TV programs, thoughts—left unchecked by biblical imperatives. . . . all are types of mental infidelity which can easily lead to trouble.[14]

The author concludes, there are no "innocent" temptations but that are enemies of a healthy marriage.

So, we must be on constant alert to the little things that become "big" things.

PRAYER: Father, keep me constantly aware of the vows I have made even as I am constantly aware of Your love for me. From the very beginning make me more sensitive to the little things that would threaten either my marriage or my relationship to You. Amen.

WHAT DOES THIS PHRASE MEAN TO YOU?

32

PHRASE: *"Forasmuch as this man and this woman have consented together in holy wedlock . . ."*

TEXT: "He who finds a wife finds what is good and receives favor from the Lord" (Prov. 18:22, NIV).

DEFINITION: consent, *v*   1. agree.

IDEA: For hundreds of years a battle raged in the church over what precisely made marriage a marriage. Some cited Paul's insistence that intercourse made a couple "one flesh." But, if intercourse made the couple "married," a lot of people were bigamists.

When women were chattels, the father's decision was considered binding, unless she eloped.

Finally, the church ruled it was consent alone.

Marriages were once used to seal political alliances. Adeheid was only eight years old when she was betrothed to Henry. How could she have given her consent? In the name of peace, a lot of things happened.

You are agreeing to be perceived as one. That is a deliberate decision—a choice. Make certain it is a wise choice.

PRAYER: Father, we believe You have led us to this point in our lives and that You will continue to lead us—whatever the future holds. Help us to realize that we can only *consent* in Your name and through the strength You give us. Amen.

WHAT DOES THIS PHRASE MEAN TO YOU?

. 33

PHRASE: "... *and have witnessed the same before God and this company* ..."

TEXT: "But you will receive power when the Holy Spirit comes on you; and you will be my witnesses in Jerusalem, and in all

Judea and Samaria, and to the ends of the earth" (Acts 1:8, NIV).

DEFINITION: same, *adj*   4. just spoken of.

IDEA: You have given the evidence of your consent to those who will sign your marriage license: the minister and the witnesses, probably best man and maid of honor. But the consent was also heard by those gathered for the ceremony.

You now become witnesses to the reality of a Christian wedding. People—some of whom are skeptical about marriage in today's world—will watch you live out and keep your vows. You vowed to
(1) cherish;
(2) honor;
(3) comfort;
(4) keep;
(5) love;
(6) keep yourself only to him/her exclusively.

In order to build a dynamic marriage, you must work equally on these vows. In fact, you won't have time to break the sexual vow if you're working on the other six.

One generation could redeem the whole concept of marriage—not just in your neighborhood or city—but all across Western civilization. Just as the disciples turned the world upside down with their witness, so can you. A Christian witness to marriage can be dynamic and life changing!

PRAYER: Father, we could have chosen to marry in a pasture or on top of a mountain. But we have chosen a place rich in our spiritual heritages. We invite You to be there—to make it more than just a wedding, but a moment of worship and celebration. Amen.

WHAT DOES THIS PHRASE MEAN TO YOU?

34

PHRASE: *". . . and have declared the same by joining of hands . . ."*

TEXT: "It is said, 'The two will become one flesh.' But he who unites himself with the Lord is one with him in spirit" (1 Cor. 6:16-17, NIV).

DEFINITION: hand, *n*   13. promise of marriage.

IDEA: Grant Silverman, in *Rome and the Romans,* reports that in early Roman times there were no formal ceremonies, or wording, or licenses. Witnesses were required to hear the consent. The emphasis was on feasting and celebrating.[15]

In early America the request for marriage was expressed, "May I have your hand in marriage?"

The hands have always been important for commitment. The word "testimony" grew out of the custom of touching each other during an oath. Before written contracts, when a man's word was final, many agreements were concluded with a "Let's shake on it." The handshake brought the promisers physically close together.

Holding hands is one of the first intimacies of a relationship; among those in love, it is never abandoned.

So, the day you are married and join hands, you continue a time-honored custom. It is the great common act for wealthy brides and grooms as well as for the poor; for the young as well as the old.

PRAYER: Father, our right hands will be joined, as a symbol of our love. Remind us of the other significant moments when our right hands have sealed decisions and commitments. Amen.

WHAT DOES THIS PHRASE MEAN TO YOU?

35

PHRASE: *". . . I pronounce that they are husband and wife together . . ."*

TEXT: "For this reason a man will leave his father and mother and will be united to his wife, and the two will become one flesh" (Eph. 5:31, NIV).

DEFINITION: pronounce, *v*   4. declare (a person or thing) to be.

IDEA: Originally, the father of the bride did the pronouncement. It was not until the 9th century that clergy became involved in weddings and then only to offer a blessing. In the 1500s the Council of Trent mandated the bishop's permission for marriage.

   The Germans, however, gave the father this right since he "owned" the daughter and literally transferred her to his son-in-law.

   You will be "husband and wife," a clarification of the original "man and wife," in an era of inclusive language. The phrase *together* acknowledges that it takes a wife to define the husband; it takes a husband to define a wife. You have to have one to have the other.

   Marriage is a harness in which both pull together.

PRAYER: Father, You who created our first parents, Adam and Eve, and sanctified and joined them together in marriage, pour out upon us the riches of Your grace. Sanctify and bless us, so that we may please You, in both body and soul, so that we may live together in holy love until our lives end. Amen.

WHAT DOES THIS PHRASE MEAN TO YOU?

36

PHRASE: *"In the name of the Father, and of the Son, and of the Holy Spirit."*

TEXT: "Whatever you do, whether in word or deed, do it all in the name of the Lord Jesus, giving thanks to God the Father through him" (Col. 3:17, NIV).

DEFINITION: name, *n*   1. with appeal to the name of.

IDEA: These words were added to weddings in 802 by order of the Emperor Charlemagne. The first weddings had been entirely civil—although some were concluded with an oath to Jupiter or Juno.

The early Christians' prayers to Jehovah were not flippant. During Nero's days, they did not know how long their marriage, or even their lives, would last. Either could be terminated by a lion or at the stake.

The benediction declares that you are married not only in the eyes of the family and the state, but also in the eyes of God.

- in the name of the Father who created marriage;
- in the name of the Son who makes us able to make a vow and is our common link;
- in the name of the Holy Spirit who will enable us to keep our vows.

The Christian cannot casually invoke the Father's name on careless choices. Marriage is one of the most significant decisions of our lives.

PRAYER: Father, we want to use Your name to conclude our act of marriage. Help us to use it carefully and in such a way that You can be praised. Amen.

WHAT DOES THIS PHRASE MEAN TO YOU?

37

PHRASE: *"Those whom God has joined together let not man put asunder."*

TEXT: "Therefore what God has joined together, let man not separate" (Matt. 19:6, NIV).

DEFINITION: asunder, *adj*   apart, separate.
   adv   in pieces; in separate parts or directions.

IDEA: This is the only direct scriptural quote in the vows (from the King James Version). It adds a note of warning.

Adultery has become standard fare in television: the soaps, prime time, comedy. Somehow we've become accustomed to it as a theme. We're no longer as offended by it and we're only a step from believing "everyone's doing it."

Startling research has been reported by the *Ladies' Home Journal* that many wives have had affairs. Perhaps, as a side effect of a women's movement we've eliminated the double standard in favor of no standard. "What's good for the goose, is good for the gander!"[16]

Paul warned about "hollow and deceptive philosophy, which depends on human tradition and the basic principles of this world" (Col. 2:8, NIV).

The word "asunder" is vividly illustrated in the account in Hebrews of the suffering of the saints: "They were stoned, they were sawn asunder" (11:37). Being separated by adultery is devastating.

PRAYER: Father, there will be times when we are tempted to forget our vows or to set them aside. Help us to remember our wedding isn't Reno or Las Vegas or some neon-lit wedding chapel. It is Your sanctuary, Your vows, Your institution, our choice. Remind us that those You join together, You also strengthen to keep the vows made. Amen.

WHAT DOES THIS PHRASE MEAN TO YOU?

Notes

1. Definitions for *gather; witness; honorable; signifying; adorn; advisedly; reverence; discretion; fear; this; forsaking; will; comfort; honor; give; worse; take; rich; cherish; part; pledge; token; constant; consent; same; hand; pronounce; name;* and *asunder* are from Charles L. Barnhart, editor, *Thorndike-Barnhart Comprehensive Desk Dictionary* (Garden City: Doubleday, 1967).

2. Definitions for *instituted; health; keep; have; join; commend; holy;* and *ordinance* are from *Webster's New World Dictionary of the American Language,* college edition (New York: World Publishing Company, 1960).

3. David R. Mace, *The Christian Response to the Sexual Revolution* (Nashville: Abingdon Press, 1970), pp. 61-62.

4. Sidney Jourard, *The Transparent Self* (Cincinnati: Van-Nostrand and Sons, 1971), p. 5.

5. "Latest Profile of America's People," *U.S. News and World Report,* 41 (September 14, 1981): 26-28.

6. Eric Segal, *Love Story* (New York: Harper and Row, 1970).

7. Dwight Small, *Dwight Small Talks About Why Marriage* (Glendale, Calif.: Regal Books, 1977), p. 5.

8. "Latest Profile," *U.S. News,* 41 (September 14, 1981): 26-28.

9. Josh McDowell, *Givers, Takers and Other Kinds of Lovers* (Wheaton, Ill.: Tyndale House, 1979).

10. Jason Towner, *Jason Loves Jane but They Got a Divorce* (Nashville: Impact Books, 1978), p. 17.

11. Ibid.

12. Jason Towner, *Warm Reflections* (Nashville: Broadman Press, 1977), p. 52.

13. Towner, *Jason Loves Jane,* p. 58.

14. Editorial, "Dads Only," Quoted in *Family Concerns,* V (October, 1981): 2.

15. Grant Silverman, *Rome and the Romans* (New York: The Macmillan Co., 1931), p. 115.

16. "Does Marriage Give Today's Women What They Really Want?" *Ladies' Home Journal,* 47 (June, 1980): 89-91.